DIGITAL NUMBER SYSTEMS

FUNDAMENTALS OF NUMBER SYSTEM

MR. K. GOKUL

i would like to dedicate this book to my Professor (MY GURUNATHAR Mrs.S.Sudha) and also thank to Notion Press for Approve my Book

Contents

Acknowledgements

I would like to express my special thanks of gratitude to my Professor Mrs.S.Sudha as well as who gave me the excellent opportunity to do this wonderful area on the Number systems, which also helped me in doing a lot of Research and I came to know about so many new things.

I am really thankful to them. Secondly, I would also like to thank my God who helped me a lot in finishing this Book . Just because of them I was able to create my Book and make it good and enjoyable experience.

CHAPTER ONE

Number System

NUMBERS :

A number is a mathematical object used to count, measure, and label. The original examples are the natural numbers 1, 2, 3, 4, and so forth. Numbers can be represented in language with number words.

NUMBER SYSTEMS:

A collection of things (usually called numbers) together with operations on those numbers and the properties that the operations satisfy.

Example: The counting numbers (1, 2, 3, ...) together with the operations of addition, subtraction, multiplication, and division and the properties they satisfy. These properties include:

* Two counting numbers can always be added to give a result that is a counting number.

* You can only subtract a counting number from another counting number and obtain a counting number as the result if the number you subtract is smaller than the number you subtract from.

The four most common number system types are:

1) Decimal number system (Base- 10)

2) Binary number system (Base- 2)

3) Octal number system (Base-8)

4) Hexadecimal number system (Base- 16)

A system for representing (that is expressing or writing) numbers of a certain type. Example: There are several systems for representing the counting numbers. These include: The usual "base ten" or "decimal" system: 1, 2, 3, ... , 10, 11, 12, ...

The technique to represent and work with numbers is called number system. Decimal number system is the most common number system. Other popular number systems include binary number system, octal number system, hexadecimal number system, etc.

ASCII

Besides numerical data, computer must be able to handle alphabets, punctuation marks, mathematical operators, special symbols, etc. that form the complete character set of English language. The complete set of characters or symbols are called alphanumeric codes. The complete alphanumeric code typically includes –

26 upper case letters

26 lower case letters

10 digits

7 punctuation marks

20 to 40 special characters

Now a computer understands only numeric values, whatever the number system used. So all characters must have a numeric equivalent called the alphanumeric code. The most widely used alphanumeric code is American Standard Code for Information Interchange (ASCII). ASCII is a 7-bit code that has 128 (27) possible codes.

CHAPTER TWO

Decimal Number System

Decimal number system is a base 10 number system having 10 digits from 0 to 9. This means that any numerical quantity can be represented using these 10 digits.

Decimal number system is also a positional value system. This means that the value of digits will depend on its position. Let us take an example to understand this.

Say we have three numbers – 734, 971 and 207. The value of 7 in all three numbers is different–

[*] In 734, value of 7 is 7 hundreds or 700 or 7 × 100 or 7 × 102

[*] In 971, value of 7 is 7 tens or 70 or 7 × 10 or 7 × 101

[*] In 207, value 0f 7 is 7 units or 7 or 7 × 1 or 7 × 100

The weightage of each position can be represented as follows –

10^5	10^4	10^3	10^2	10^1	10^0

In digital systems, instructions are given through electric signals; variation is done by varying the voltage of the signal. Having 10 different voltages to implement decimal number system in digital equipment is difficult. So, many number systems that are easier to implement digitally have been developed. Let's look at them in detail.

Step 1 – Divide the decimal number to be converted by the value of the new base.

Step 2 – Get the remainder from Step 1 as the rightmost digit (least significant digit) of new base number.

Step 3 – Divide the quotient of the previous divide by the new base.

How do you convert a decimal?

To convert a decimal to a fraction, place the decimal number over its place value. For example, in 0.6, the six is in the tenths place, so we place 6 over 10 to create the equivalent fraction, 6/10. If needed, simplify the fraction.

CHAPTER THREE

Binary Number System

* The easiest way to vary instructions through electric signals is two-state system – on and off. On is represented as 1 and off as 0, though 0 is not actually no signal but signal at a lower voltage.

* The number system having just these two digits – 0 and 1 – is called binary number system.

* Each binary digit is also called a bit. Binary number system is also positional value system, where each digit has a value expressed in powers of 2, as displayed here.

[A number system where a number is represented by using only two digits (0 and 1) with a base 2 is called a binary number system. For example, 10012 is a binary number.]

Each binary digit is also called a **bit**. Binary number system is also positional value system, where each digit has a value expressed in powers of 2, as displayed here.

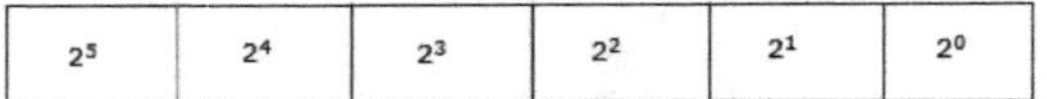

In any binary number, the rightmost digit is called **least significant bit (LSB)** and leftmost digit is called **most significant bit (MSB)**.

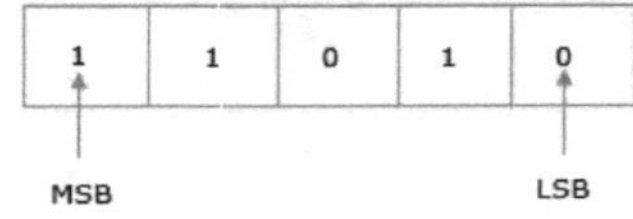

And decimal equivalent of this number is sum of product of each digit with its positional value.

$11010_2 = 1\times2^4 + 1\times2^3 + 0\times2^2 + 1\times2^1 + 0\times2^0$

$= 16 + 8 + 0 + 2 + 0$

$= 26_{10}$

binary number system, in mathematics, positional numeral system employing 2 as the base and so requiring only two different symbols for its digits, 0 and 1, instead of the usual 10 different symbols needed in the decimal system.

A binary number system is one of the four types of number system. In computer applications, where binary numbers are represented by only two symbols or digits, i.e. 0 (zero) and 1(one). The binary numbers here are expressed in the base-2 numeral system. For example, (101)2 is a binary number.

What is the formula of binary number system?

The Binary Numbering System contains only 0's and 1's. A binary number such as 101100101 is expressed with a string of 0's and 1's with each digit having a value twice that of the previous digit.

Why is binary 1 or 0?

Because there are only two valid Boolean values for representing either a logic “1” or a logic “0”, makes the system of using Binary Numbers ideal for use in digital or electronic circuits and systems.

Who defined the binary system :Gottfried Wilhelm Leibniz

Gottfried Wilhelm Leibniz (1646-1716) is the self-proclaimed inventor of the binary system and is considered as such by most historians of mathematics and/or mathematicians.

Why is binary important?

Binary numbers are important because using them instead of the decimal system simplifies the design of computers and related technologies.

NOTE:

A binary number is a number expressed in the base-2 numeral system or binary numeral system, a method of mathematical expression which uses only two symbols: typically "0" and "1". The base-2 numeral system is a positional notation with a radix of 2. Each digit is referred to as a bit, or binary digit.

Computer memory is measured in terms of how many bits it can store. Here is a chart for memory capacity conversion.

1 byte (B) = 8 bits

1 Kilobytes (KB) = 1024 bytes

1 Megabyte (MB) = 1024 KB

1 Gigabyte (GB) = 1024 MB

1 Terabyte (TB) = 1024 GB

1 Exabyte (EB) = 1024 PB

1 Zettabyte = 1024 EB

1 Yottabyte (YB) = 1024 ZB

CHAPTER FOUR

Octal Number System

Octal number system has eight digits – 0, 1, 2, 3, 4, 5, 6 and 7. Octal number system is also a positional value system with where each digit has its value expressed in powers of 8, as shown here –

8^5	8^4	8^3	8^2	8^1	8^0

Decimal equivalent of any octal number is sum of product of each digit with its positional value.

$726_8 = 7\times8^2 + 2\times8^1 + 6\times8^0$

$= 448 + 16 + 6$

$= 470_{10}$

A number system which has its base as 'eight' is called an Octal number system. It uses numbers from 0 to 7. Let us take an example, to understand the concept. As we said, any number with base 8 is an octal number like 248, 1098, 558, etc

The octal numeral system, or oct for short, is the base-8 number system, and uses the digits 0 to 7, that is to say 10octal represents eight and 100octal represents sixty-four.

However, English, like most languages, uses a base-10 number system, hence a true octal system might use different vocabulary.

What is octal number system used for?

What are the Uses of Octal Numbers? The Octal Number system is widely used in computer application sectors and digital numbering systems. The computing systems use 16-bit, 32-bit or 64-bit word which is further divided into 8-bits words. The octal number is also used in the aviation sector in the form of a code.

How do you represent 8 in octal?

Octal numbers therefore have a range of just "8" digits, (0, 1, 2, 3, 4, 5, 6, 7) making them a Base-8 numbering system and therefore, q is equal to "8".

Convert Decimal to Octal with Steps

STEP 1: Write the given decimal number.

STEP 2: If the given decimal number is less than 8 the octal number is the same.

STEP 3:If the decimal number is greater than 7 then divide the number by 8.

STEP 4:Note the remainder, we get after division.

Octal Number System is one the type of Number Representation techniques, in which there value of base is 8. That means there are only 8 symbols or possible digit values, there are 0, 1, 2, 3, 4, 5, 6, 7. It requires only 3 bits to represent value of any digit. Octal numbers are indicated by the addition of either an 0o prefix or an 8 suffix.

Position of every digit has a weight which is a power of 8. Each position in the Octal system is 8 times more significant than the previous position, that means numeric value of an octal number is determined by multiplying each digit of the number by the value of the position in which the digit appears and then adding the products. So, it is also a positional (or weighted) number system.

Representation of Octal Number

Each Octal number can be represented using only 3 bits, with each group of bits having a distich values between 000 (for 0) and 111 (for 7 = 4+2+1).

Most Significant Bit (MSB)	Octal Point		Least Significant Bit (LSB)		
8^2	8^1	8^0	8^{-1}	8^{-2}	8^{-3}
64	8	1	1/8	1/64	1/512

Since base value of Octal number system is 8, so there maximum value of digit is 7 and it can not be more than 7. In this number system, the successive positions to the left of the octal point having weights of 8^0, 8^1, 8^2, 8^3 and so on. Similarly, the successive positions to the right of the octal point having weights of 8^{-1}, 8^{-2}, $8^{-3}$and so on. This is called base power of 8. The decimal value of any octal number can be determined using sum of product of each digit with its positional value.

Example-1 – The number 111 is interpreted as

111 = 1x82+5x81+7x80 = 157

Here, right most bit 7 is the least significant bit (LSB) and left most bit 1 is the most significant bit (MSB).

Example-2 – The number 65.125 is interpreted as

65.125 =1x82+0x81+1x80+1x8-1=101.10

Here, right most bit 0 is the least significant bit (LSB) and left most bit 1 is the most significant bit (MSB).

Advantages and Disadvantages

The main advantage of using Octal numbers is that it uses less digits than decimal and Hexadecimal number system. So, it has fewer computations and less computational errors. It uses only 3 bits to represent any digit in binary and easy to convert from octal to binary and vice-versa. It is easier to handle input and output in the octal form.

The major disadvantage of Octal number system is that computer does not understand octal number system directly, so we need octal to binary converter.

Applications of Octal Number System

The octal numbers are not as common as they used to be. However, Octal is used when the number of bits in one word is a multiple of 3. It is also used as a shorthand for representing file permissions on UNIX systems and representation of UTF8 numbers, etc.

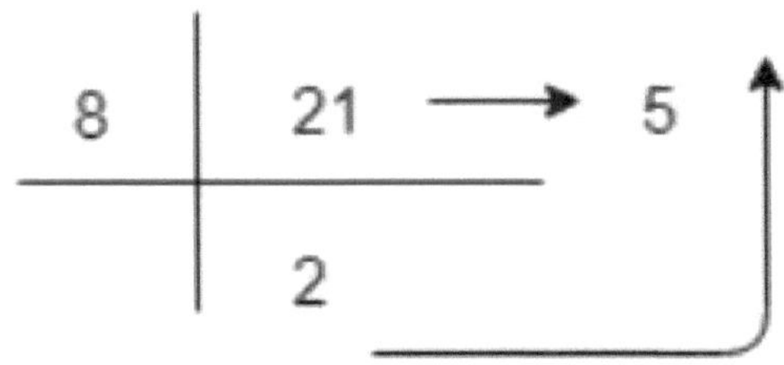

(21)10=2x81+5x80=(25)8 So, decimal value 21 is equivalent to 25 in Octal Number System.

Octal Numbering System (base 8)

Characters = 0,1,2,3,4,5,6,7

4 3 7 = 4x64+ 3x8 + 7x1

64's place 8's place 1's place

written 437_o or 437_8

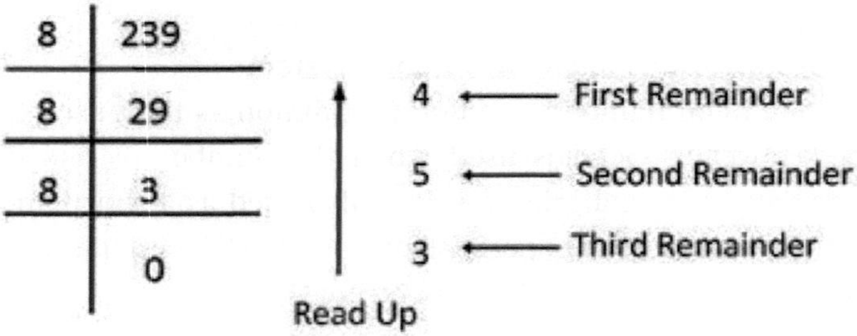

8	239
8	29
8	3
	0

4 ← First Remainder

5 ← Second Remainder

3 ← Third Remainder

↑ Read Up

CONVERSION II

CHAPTER FIVE

Hexadecimal Number System

What is a hexadecimal number system?

* The hexadecimal number system is a number system with base-16. It is represented by only 16 digits or values

* Octal number system has 16 symbols – 0 to 9 and A to F where A is equal to 10, B is equal to 11 and so on till F. Hexadecimal number system is also a positional value system with where each digit has its value expressed in powers of 16, as shown here –

16^5	16^4	16^3	16^2	16^1	16^0

Hexadecimal

Decimal equivalent of any hexadecimal number is sum of product of each digit with its positional value.

27FB16 = 2×163 + 7×162 + 15×161 + 10×160

= 8192 + 1792 + 240 +10

= 1023410

Hexadecimal is a numbering system with base 16. It can be used to represent large numbers with fewer digits. In this system there are 16 symbols or possible digit values from 0 to 9, followed by six alphabetic characters -- A, B, C, D, E and F.

What is hexadecimal number system with example?

It is also pronounced sometimes as 'hex'. Hexadecimal numbers are represented by only 16 symbols. These symbols or values are 0, 1, 2, 3, 4, 5, 6, 7, 8, 9, A, B, C, D, E and F. Each digit represents a decimal value. For example, D is equal to base-10 13.

How do you write 16 in hexadecimal?

This makes conversion between binary and hexadecimal numbers very easy, and hexadecimal can be used to write large binary numbers with much fewer digits.

What hexadecimal means?

Hexadecimal is a numbering system with base 16. It can be used to represent large numbers with fewer digits. In this system there are 16 symbols or possible digit values from 0 to 9, followed by six alphabetic characters -- A, B, C, D, E and F

How many colors are there in hex?

How Many Hex Colors Are There? In standard #RRGGBB notation, there are 256^3 color combinations available, or 16,777,216. This is because each color value RR, GG, BB can contain 256 different values, ranging from 00 to FF. Therefore, the number of combinations is 256^3.

Hexadecimal Number System is one the type of Number Representation techniques, in which there value of base is 16. That means there are only 16 symbols or possible digit values, there are 0, 1, 2, 3, 4, 5, 6, 7, 8, 9, A, B, C, D, E, F. Where A, B, C, D, E and F are single bit representations of decimal value 10, 11, 12, 13, 14 and 15 respectively.

It requires only 4 bits to represent value of any digit. Hexadecimal numbers are indicated by the addition of either an 0x prefix or an h suffix.

Position of every digit has a weight which is a power of 16. Each position in the Hexadecimal system is 16 times more significant than the previous position, that means numeric value of an hexadecimal number is determined by multiplying each digit of the number by the value of the position in which the digit appears and then adding the products. So, it is also a positional (or weighted) number system.

Representation of Hexadecimal Number

Each Hexadecimal number can be represented using only 4 bits, with each group of bits having a distich values between 0000 (for 0) and 1111 (for F = 15 = 8+4+2+1). The equivalent binary number of Hexadecimal number are as given below.

Hex digit	1	0	2	3	4	5	6	7
Binary	0000	0001	0010	0011	0100	0101	0110	0111

Hex digit	8	9	A = 10	B = 11	C = 12	D = 13	E = 14	F = 15
Binary	1000	1001	1010	1011	1100	1101	1110	1111

Hexadecimal number system is similar to Octal number system. Hexadecimal number system provides convenient way of converting large binary numbers into more compact and smaller groups.

Most Significant Bit (MSB)	Hex Point		Least Significant Bit (LSB)		
16^2	16^1	16^0	16^{-1}	16^{-2}	16^{-3}
256	16	1	1/16	1/256	1/4096

Since base value of Hexadecimal number system is 16, so there maximum value of digit is 15 and it can not be more than 15. In this number system, the successive positions to the left of the hexadecimal point having weights of 160, 161, 162, 163and so on. Similarly, the successive positions to the right of the hexadecimal point having weights of 16-1, 16-2, 16-3and so on. This is called base power of 16. The decimal value of any hexadecimal number can be determined using sum of product of each digit with its positional value.

Example-1 – The number 512 is interpreted as

512=2x162+0x161+0x160=200

Here, right most bit 0 is the least significant bit (LSB) and left most bit 2 is the most significant bit (MSB).

Example-2 – The number 2015.0625 is interpreted as

2015.0625=7x162+13x161+15x160+1x16-1=7DF.10

Here, right most bit 0 is the least significant bit (LSB) and left most bit 7 is the most significant bit (MSB).

Example-3 A a decimal number 21 to represent in Hexadecimal representation

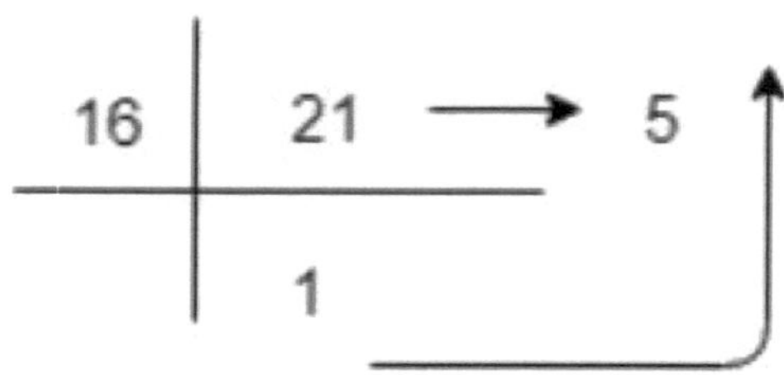

(21)10=1x161+5x160=(15)16 So, decimal value 21 is equivalent to 15 in Hexadecimal Number System.

Applications of Hexadecimal Number System

Hexadecimal Number System is commonly used in Computer programming and Microprocessors. It is also helpful to describe colors on web pages. Each of the three primary colors (i.e., red, green and blue) is represented by two hexadecimal digits to create 255 possible values, thus resulting in more than 16 million possible colors. Hexadecimal number system is used to describe locations in memory for every byte. These hexadecimal numbers are also easier to read and write than binary or decimal numbers for Computer Professionals.

Advantages and Disadvantages

The main advantage of using Hexadecimal numbers is that it uses less memory to store more numbers, for example it store 256 numbers in two digits whereas decimal number stores 100 numbers in two digits. This number system is also used to represent Computer memory addresses. It uses only 4 bits to represent any digit in binary and easy to convert from hexadecimal to binary and vice-versa. It is easier to handle input and output in the hexadecimal form. There is wide number of advantages in data science field, artificial intelligence and machine learning.

The major disadvantage of Hexadecimal number system is that it may not an easy to read and write for people, and also difficult to perform operations like multiplications, divisions using hexadecimal number system. Hexadecimal numbers is most difficult number system for dealing with Computer's data.

15's and 16's Complement of Hexadecimal (Base-16) Number

Simply, 15's complement of a hexadecimal number is the subtraction of it's each digits from F(=15). For example, 15's complement of hexadecimal number 2030 is FFFF - 2030 = DFCF.

16's complement of hexadecimal number is 15's complement of given number plus 1 to the least significant bit (LSB). For example 8's complement of hexadecimal number 2020 is (FFFF - 2030) + 1 = DFDF + 1 = DFE0. Please note that maximum digit of hexadecimal number system is F(=15), so addition of F+1 will be 0 with carry 1.

CHAPTER SIX

Number System Relationship

The technique to represent and work with numbers is called number system. Decimal number system is the most common number system. Other popular number systems include binary number system, octal number system, hexadecimal number system, etc.

Definition: A number base is the number of digits or combination of digits that a system of counting uses to represent numbers. A base can be any whole number greater than 0. The most commonly used number system is the decimal system, commonly known as base 10.

What are number relations?

Number relationships, which go far beyond counting skills, refer to the ability to represent a quantity in multiple, flexible ways. It is arguably among the most important mathematics concepts in number and quantity.

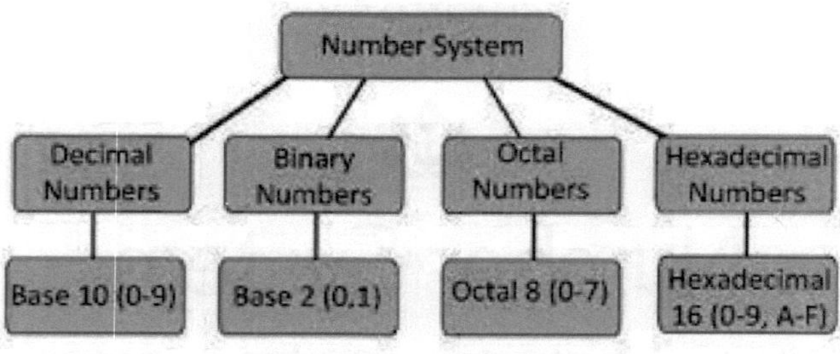

Decimal	Binary	Octal	Hexadecimal
0	0000	000	0000
1	0001	001	0001
2	0010	002	0002
3	0011	003	0003
4	0100	004	0004
5	0101	005	0005
6	0110	006	0006
7	0111	007	0007
8	1000	010	0008
9	1001	011	0009
10	1010	012	A
11	1011	013	B
12	1100	014	C
13	1101	015	D
14	1110	016	E
15	1111	017	F

CHAPTER SEVEN

ASCII

Besides numerical data, computer must be able to handle alphabets, punctuation marks, mathematical operators, special symbols, etc. that form the complete character set of English language.

The complete set of characters or symbols are called alphanumeric codes. The complete alphanumeric code typically includes –

26 upper case letters

26 lower case letters

10 digits

7 punctuation marks

20 to 40 special characters

Now a computer understands only numeric values, whatever the number system used. So all characters must have a numeric equivalent called the alphanumeric code. The most widely used alphanumeric code is American Standard Code for Information Interchange (ASCII). ASCII is a 7-bit code that has 128 (27) possible codes.

ASCII Code - Character to Binary

0	0011 0000	I	0100 1001	b	0110 0010	v	0111 0110
1	0011 0001	J	0100 1010	c	0110 0011	w	0111 0111
2	0011 0010	K	0100 1011	d	0110 0100	x	0111 1000
3	0011 0011	L	0100 1100	e	0110 0101	y	0111 1001
4	0011 0100	M	0100 1101	f	0110 0110	z	0111 1010
5	0011 0101	N	0100 1110	g	0110 0110		
6	0011 0110	O	0100 1111	h	0110 1000	:	0011 1010
7	0011 0110	P	0101 0000	i	0110 1001	;	0011 1011
8	0011 1000	Q	0101 0001	j	0110 1010	?	0011 1111
9	0011 1001	R	0101 0010	k	0110 1011	.	0010 1110
		S	0101 0011	l	0110 1100	'	0010 1111
A	0100 0001	T	0101 0100	m	0110 1101	!	0010 0001
B	0100 0010	U	0101 0101	n	0110 1110	,	0010 1100
C	0100 0011	V	0101 0110	o	0110 1111	"	0010 0010
D	0100 0100	W	0101 0111	p	0111 0000	(	0010 1000
E	0100 0101	X	0101 1000	q	0111 0001	)	0010 1001
F	0100 0110	Y	0101 1001	r	0111 0010	space	0010 0000
G	0100 0111	Z	0101 1010	s	0111 0011		
H	0100 1000			t	0111 0100		
		a	0110 0001	u	0111 0101		

ISCII

ISCII stands for Indian Script Code for Information Interchange. IISCII was developed to support Indian languages on computer. Language supported by IISCI include Devanagari, Tamil, Bangla, Gujarati, Gurmukhi, Tamil, Telugu, etc. IISCI is mostly used by government departments and before it could catch on, a new universal encoding standard called Unicode was introduced.

Unicode

Unicode is an international coding system designed to be used with different language scripts. Each character or symbol is assigned a unique numeric value, largely within the framework of ASCII. Earlier, each script had its own encoding system, which could conflict with each other.

In contrast, this is what Unicode officially aims to do – Unicode provides a unique number for every character, no matter what the platform, no matter what the program, no matter what the language.

As you know decimal, binary, octal and hexadecimal number systems are positional value number systems. To convert binary, octal and hexadecimal to decimal number, we just need to add the product of each digit with its positional value. Here we are going to learn other conversion among these number systems

CHAPTER EIGHT

Decimal to Binary

Decimal numbers can be converted to binary by repeated division of the number by 2 while recording the remainder. Let's take an example to see how this happens.

Decimal	Binary
1	0
2	10
3	11
4	100
5	101
6	110
7	111
8	1000
9	1001
10	1010

		Remainder	
2	43		
2	21	1	MSB ↑
2	10	1	
2	5	0	
2	2	1	
2	1	0	
	0	1	LSB

The remainders are to be read from bottom to top to obtain the binary equivalent.

4310 = 1010112

EXAMPLE CONVERSION:

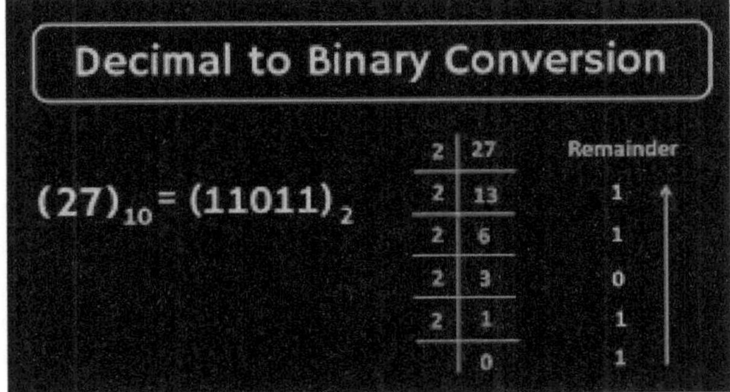

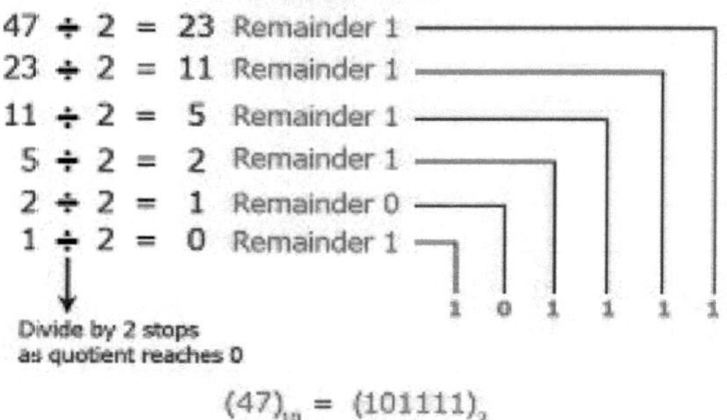

$(160)_{10}$

2	160	
2	80	0
2	40	0
2	20	0
2	10	0
2	5	0
2	2	1
	1	0

CHAPTER NINE

Decimal to Octal

Decimal numbers can be converted to octal by repeated division of the number by 8 while recording the remainder. Let's take an example to see how this happens

Divisor	Number	**Remainder**	
8	473		
8	59	1	**MSD**
8	7	3	↑
	0	7	**LSD**

Reading the remainders from bottom to top,
47310 = 7318

Decimal number	Octal number
0	0
1	1
2	2
3	3
4	4
5	5
6	6
7	7
8	10
9	11
10	12
11	13
12	14
13	15
14	16
15	17
16	20

EXAMPLE CONVERSION

	1486	
8	185	-6
8	23	-1
8	2	-7

2	45	 1
2	22	 0
2	11	 1
2	5	 1
2	2	 0
	1	

$$\therefore 45_{10} = 101101_2$$

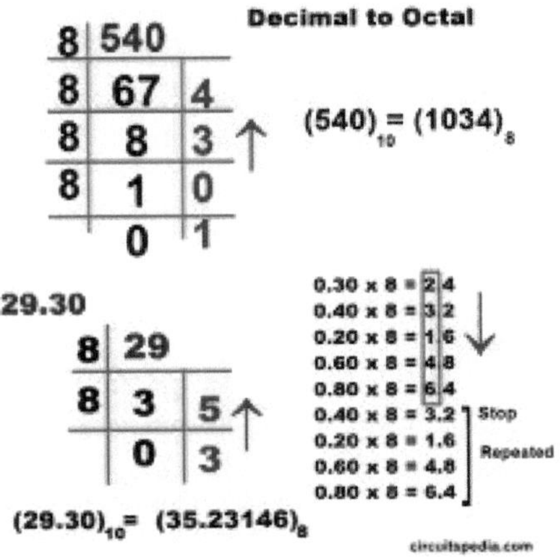

8	350		
8	43	----- 6	↑ Remainder
	5	----- 3	

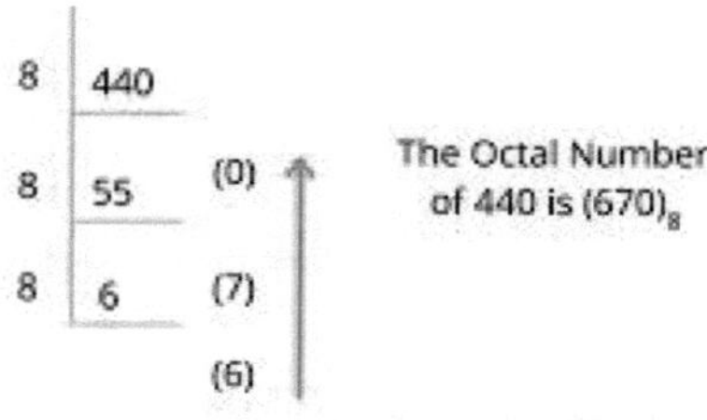

2018
-1536 (3 x 512)
482
- 448 (7 x 64)
34
- 32 (4 x 8)
2
- 2 (2 x 1)
0

8^4	8^3	8^2	8^1	8^0
4096	512	64	8	1
	3	7	4	2

Answer: 2018_{10} = $\mathbf{3742_8}$

CHAPTER TEN

Decimal to Hexadecimal

Decimal numbers can be converted to octal by repeated division of the number by 16 while recording the remainder. Let's take an example to see how this happens.

		Remainder
16	423	
16	26	7
16	1	A
	0	1

Reading the remainders from bottom to top we get,
42310 = 1A716
EXAMPLE CONVERSION:

Decimal Number: 2545

16 | 2545   1 <10, arr[0] = 1

16 | 159   15 >10, arr[1] = F

16 | 9   9 < 10, arr[2] = 9

0

remainder

Hexadecimal number: 41

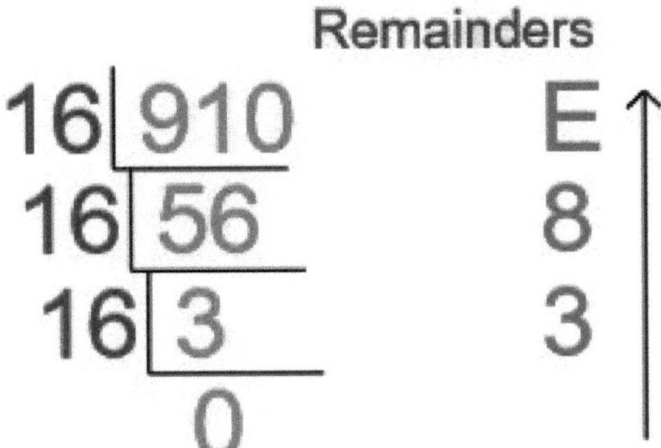

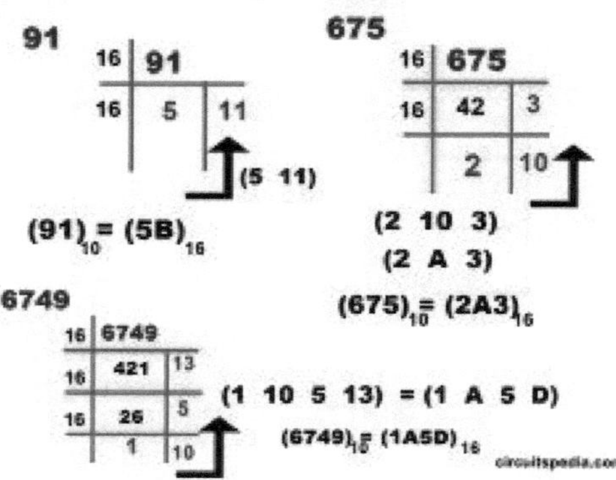
Decimal to Hexadecimal
91
16 91
16 5 11
(5 11)
(91)10 = (5B)16
675
16 675
16 42 3
2 10
(2 10 3)
(2 A 3)
(675)10 = (2A3)16
6749
16 6749
16 421 13
16 26 5
1 10
(1 10 5 13) = (1 A 5 D)
(6749)10 = (1A5D)16
circuitspedia.com

CHAPTER ELEVEN

Binary to Octal

Conversion from Binary to Octal

STEP 1 :Take the given binary number.

STEP 2: Multiply each digit by 2n-1 where n is the position of the digit from the decimal.

STEP3 :The resultant is the equivalent decimal number for the given binary number.

STEP 4: Divide the decimal number by 8.

STEP5 : Note the remainder.

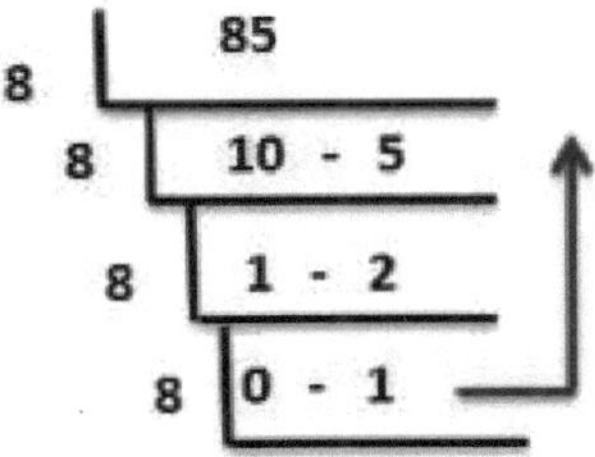

To convert an octal number to binary, each octal digit is converted to its 3-bit binary equivalent according to this table.

Octal Digit	0	1	2	3	4	5	6	7
Binary Equivalent	000	001	010	011	100	101	110	111

$54673_8 = 101100110111011_2$

Binary to Octal Conversion

$(1101011.00101)_2$

1101011.00101

Binary	Octal
000	0
001	1
010	2
011	3
100	4
101	5
110	6
111	7

To convert binary numbers into octal ones, you only have to make 3-bit groups and convert directly each group:

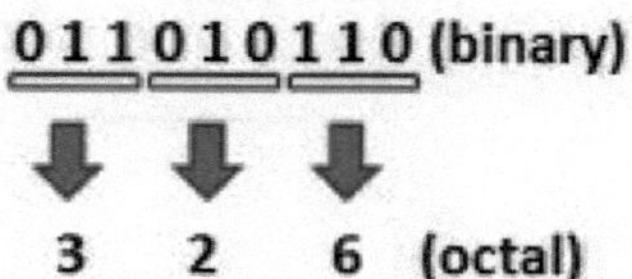

Enter Caption

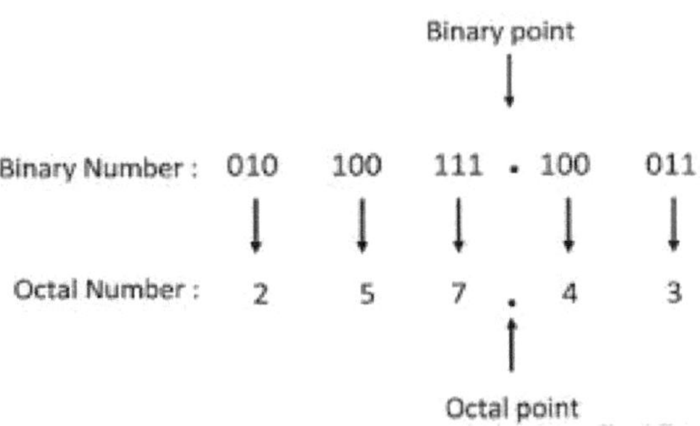

Binary to Octal Conversion in Python

To convert binary numbers into octal ones, you have to make 3-bit groups and convert directly each group with their respective octal number(0-7).

Hence, $(010101111)_2 = (257)_8$

CHAPTER TWELVE

Binary to Hexadecimal

To convert a binary number to hexadecimal number, these steps are followed –

STEP1 : Starting from the least significant bit, make groups of four bits.

STEP2 ; If there are one or two bits less in making the groups, 0s can be added after the most significant bit.

STEP3 : Convert each group into its equivalent octal number.

Let's take an example to understand this.

Example –

Convert binary number 1101010 into hexadecimal number.

First convert this into decimal number: = (1101010)2 = 1x26+1x25+0x24+1x23+0x22+1x21+0x20 = 64+32+0+8+0+2+0 = (106)10

Then, convert it into hexadecimal number = (106)10 = 6x161+10x160 = (6A)16 .

Number	0	1	2	3	4	5	6	7
Binary	0000	0001	0010	0011	0100	0101	0110	0111
Hexadecimal	0	1	2	3	4	5	6	7

Number	8	9	10	11	12	13	14	15
Binary	1000	1001	1010	1011	1100	1101	1110	1111
Hexadecimal	8	9	A	B	C	D	E	F

To convert binary numbers into hexadecimals, you only have to make 4-bit groups and convert directly each group:

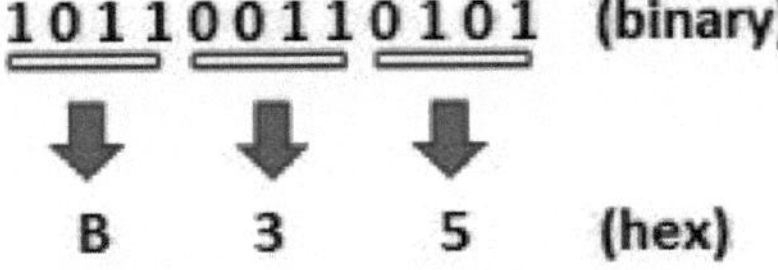

Converting Hex to Binary

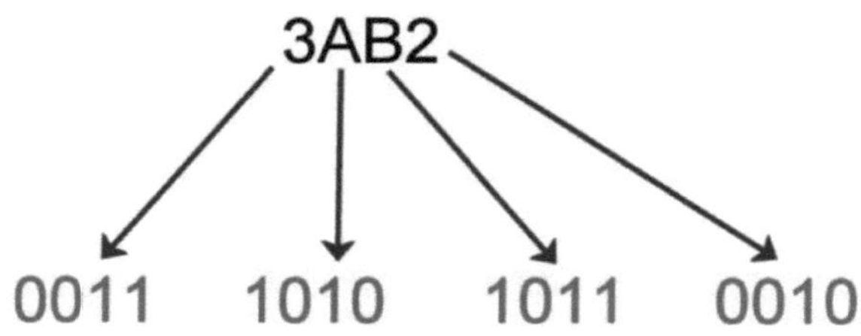

$3AB2_{16} = 11101010110010_2$

Break into nibbles: 1100 0011. 1100 = hexadecimal C and 0011 = hexadecimal 3. Remember, this is hexadecimal base 16 symbol 3, not denary symbol 3. Break into nibbles: 0011 0011

CHAPTER THIRTEEN

Binary to Decimal

To convert a binary integer to decimal,

STEP1 :start by adding the left-most digit to 0.

Step 2 :Next, multiply this by 2, and add the next digit in your number (as you progress from left to right) to this product. (In other words, multiply the current product in each step by 2 and add the current digit).

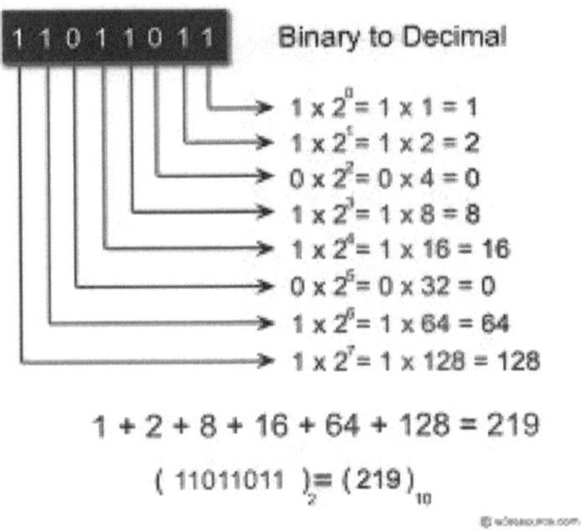

Enter Caption

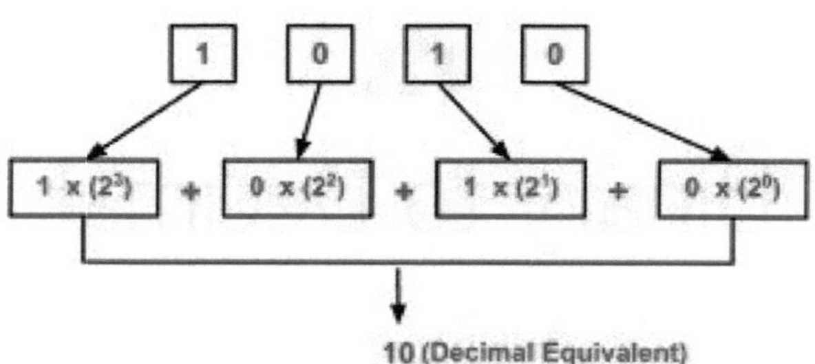
Binary number - 1010
1
0
1
0
1 x (2³) + 0 x (2²) + 1 x (2¹) + 0 x (2⁰)
10 (Decimal Equivalent)

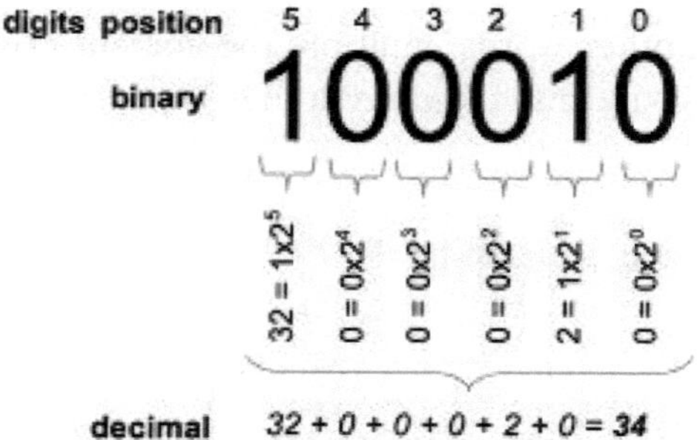
digits position
5 4 3 2 1 0
binary
100010
32 = 1x2⁵
0 = 0x2⁴
0 = 0x2³
0 = 0x2²
2 = 1x2¹
0 = 0x2⁰
decimal
32 + 0 + 0 + 0 + 2 + 0 = 34

Conversion from Binary to Decimal number system

There are mainly two methods to convert a binary number into decimal number – using positional notation, and using doubling. These methods are explained are as following below.

Using Positional Notation

Since number numbers are type of positional number system. That means weight of the positions from right to left are as 2^0, 2^1, 2^2, 2^3... and so on for the integer part and weight of the positions from left to right are as 2^{-1}, 2^{-2}, 2^{-3}, 2^{-4}... and so on for the fractional part.

Most Significant Bit (MSB)	Binary Point		Least Significant Bit (LSB)		
2^2	2^1	2^0	2^{-1}	2^{-2}	2^{-3}
4	2	1	0.5	0.25	0.125

Assume any unsigned binary number is $b_n b_{(n-1)} \dots b_1 b_0 . b_{-1} b_{-2} \dots b_{(m-1)} b_m$. Then the decimal number is equal to the sum of binary digits (b_n) times their power of 2 (2^n), i.e., $b_n b_{(n-1)} \dots b_1 b_0 . b_{-1} b_{-2} \dots b_{(m-1)} b_m = b_n x2^n + b_{(n-1)} x2^{(n-1)} + \dots + b_1 x2^1 + bx_0 2^0 + b_{-1} x2^{-1} + b_{-2} 2^{-2} +$

Binary to decimal is,

= (11001010)2

= 1x27+1x26+0x25+0x24+1x23+0x22+1x21+0x20

= 128+64+0+0+8+0+2+0

= (202)10

Convert binary number 11101110 into decimal number.

According to above algorithm, Binary to decimal is,

= (11101110)2

= 1

= 12+1

=3

= 32+1

=7

= 72+0

=14

= 142+1

=29

= 292+1

=59

= 592+1

=119

= 1192+0

=238

= (238)10

CHAPTER FOURTEEN

Octal to Decimal

Octal to Decimal conversion is just like the other conversions in the number system such as decimal to octal, octal to hexadecimal, octal to binary, and so on. Octal to decimal conversion occurs when an octal number with the base of 8 has to be converted to a decimal number with the base of 10. Let us learn more about the conversion methods and solve a few examples for a better understanding.

Step 1: Since an octal number only uses digits from 0 to 7, we first arrange the octal number with the power of 8.

Step 2: We evaluate all the power of 8 values such as 80 is 1, 81 is 8, etc., and write down the value of each octal number.

Step 3: Once the value is obtained, we multiply each number.

Step 4: Final step is to add the product of all the numbers to obtain the decimal number.

Let us look at an example, convert (140)8(140)8 into a decimal number.

Step 1: Write 140 with the power of 8. Start from the right-hand side.

1 × 82 + 4 × 81 + 0 × 80

Step 2: Evaluate the power of 8 values for each octal number.

82 = 64, 81 = 8, 80 = 1

Step 3: Multiply each of the power of 8 numbers with the respective numbers.

$1 \times 64 + 4 \times 8 + 0 \times 1 = 64 + 32 + 0$

Step 4: Add the values to obtain the decimal number.

$64 + 32 + 0 = 96.$

Therefore, (140)8(140)8 = (96)10(96)10.

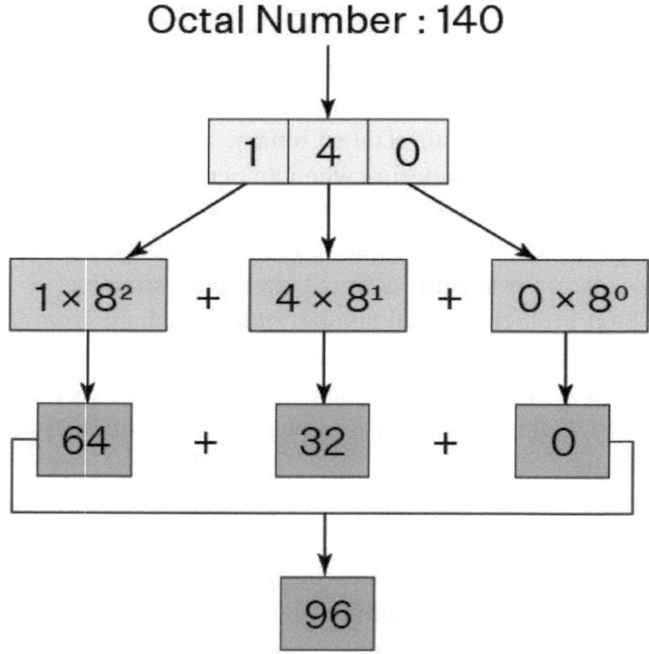

$(140)_8 = (96)_{10}$

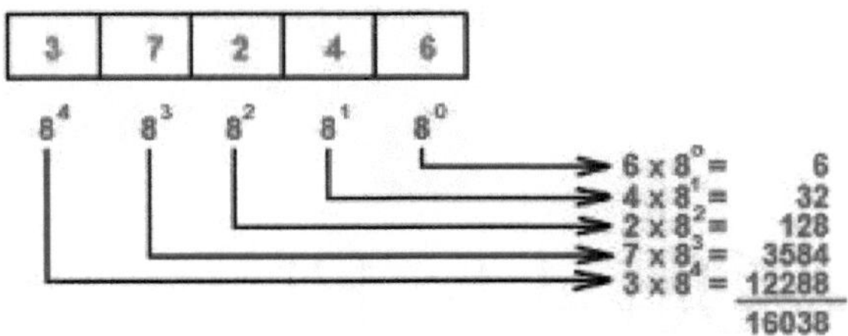

Octal = 37246

Decimal = 16038

CHAPTER FIFTEEN

Octal to Binary

Octal number is one of the number systems which has value of base is 8, that means there only 8 symbols – 0, 1, 2, 3, 4, 5, 6, and 7.

Whereas Binary number is most familiar number system to the digital systems, networking, and computer professionals. It is base 2 which has only 2 symbols – 0 and 1, these digits can be represented by off and on respectively.

Conversion from Octal to Binary number system

There are various direct or indirect methods to convert a octal number into binary number. In an indirect method, you need to convert an octal number into other number system (e.g., decimal or hexadecimal), then you can convert into binary number by converting each digit into binary number from hexadecimal system and using conversion system from decimal to binary number.

Octal Symbol	Binary equivalent
0	000
1	001
2	010
3	011
4	100
5	101
6	110
7	111

This method is simple and also works as reverse of Binary to Octal Conversion. The algorithm is explained as following below.

- Take Octal number as input
- Convert each digit of octal into binary.
- That will be output as binary number.

Example-1 Convert octal number 540 into binary number.

According to above algorithm, equivalent binary number will be,

= (540)8

= (101 100 000)2

= (101100000)2

This is very simple conversion, you can use for mixed (integer with fractional) octal number as well.

Example-2 – Convert octal number 352.563 into binary number.

According to above algorithm, equivalent binary number will be,

= (352.563)8

= (011 101 010 . 101 110 011)2

= (011101010.101110011)2

<u>Octal Number System:</u>

The octal numeral system, or oct for short, is the base-8 number system, and uses the digits 0 to 7. Octal numerals can be made from binary numerals by grouping consecutive binary digits into groups of three (starting from the right).

Binary Number System:

In mathematics and digital electronics, a binary number is a number expressed in the binary numeral system or base-2 numeral system which represents numeric values using two different symbols: typically 0 (zero) and 1 (one). The base-2 system is a positional notation with a radix of 2. Because of its straightforward implementation in digital electronic circuitry using logic gates, the binary system is used internally by almost all modern computers and computer-based devices. Each digit is referred to as a bit.

CHAPTER SIXTEEN

Octal to Hexadecimal

In mathematics and computing, hexadecimal (also base 16, or hex) is a positional numeral system with a radix, or base, of 16.

Octal Number System:

The octal numeral system, or oct for short, is the base-8 number system, and uses the digits 0 to 7. Octal numerals can be made from binary numerals by grouping consecutive binary digits into groups of three (starting from the right).

Hexadecimal Number System:

In mathematics and computing, hexadecimal (also base 16, or hex) is a positional numeral system with a radix, or base, of 16. It uses sixteen distinct symbols, most often the symbols 0–9 to represent values zero to nine, and A,B,C,D,E,F (or alternatively a, b, c, d, e, f) to represent values ten to fifteen.

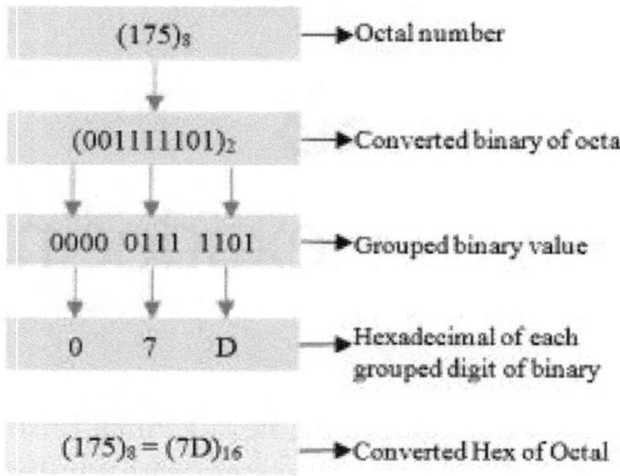

What are Octal Numbers?

Octal numbers have base 8. These numbers use digits from 0 to 7, total 8 digits and hence, they are called octal number system. Octal numbers have base 8. It is denoted as o8 and o is an octal number. It does not use digits 8 and 9 to represent a number.

Example: (112)8, (275)8,(45)8

Hexadecimal to Octal Conversion

Conversion of hexadecimal to octal cannot be done directly. Firstly we need to convert hexadecimal into its equivalent decimal number then decimal to octal. Follow the steps below to understand the process.

step 1: Consider the given hexadecimal number

step 2 :First count the number of digits in the number

step 3: If n is the position of the digit from the right end then multiply each digit with 16n-1

step 4: Add the terms after multiplication

step 5: Resultant is the equivalent decimal form

step 6: Divide the decimal number with 8

step 7: Note down the remainder

step8 : Repeat the previous two steps with the quotient, until the quotient is zero

step 9: Write the remainders in reverse order

step 10:The obtained number is the required result

Hexadecimal	Octal	Equivalent Decimal	Equivalent BInary
0	0	0	0
1	1	1	1
2	2	2	10
3	3	3	11
4	4	4	100
5	5	5	101
6	6	6	110
7	7	7	111
8	10	8	1000
9	11	9	1001
A	12	10	1010
B	13	11	1011
C	14	12	1100
D	15	13	1101
E	16	14	1110

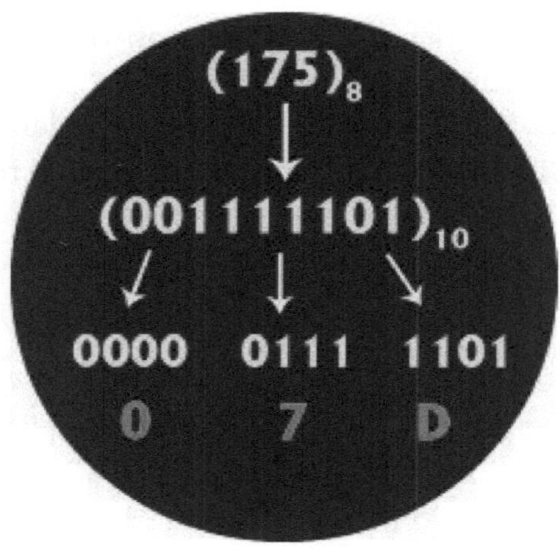
(175)8
(001111101)10
0000 0111 1101
0 7 D

CHAPTER SEVENTEEN

Hexadecimal to Binary

Binary Numbers:

The number which uses only the digits 0 and 1 and data in this system will be the combination of 0's and 1's. It uses only 2 digits so it is called binary numbers. It is denoted by b2, where b is any binary number.

Examples: 1) 0101112 2) 001110112 3) 1112

Hexadecimal Number:

Hexa means 16. In the hexadecimal number system, it uses 16 digits. It consists of numbers and alphabets. It includes numbers 0, 1, 2, 3, 4, 5, 6, 7, 8, 9 and A, B, C, D, E, F; total 16 digits. It is denoted by s16, where s is a hexadecimal number.

Convert every hex digit (start lowest digit) to 4 binary digits, with this table:

Hex	Binary
0	0000
1	0001
2	0010
3	0011
4	0100
5	0101
6	0110
7	0111
8	1000
9	1001
A	1010
B	1011
C	1100
D	1101
E	1110
F	1111

Example

Convert hex 6C16 to binary:

6C16 = 6 C = 110 1100 = 11011002

How to Convert Hexadecimal to Binary Number?

To convert a hexadecimal number into its equivalent binary number, follow the steps given here:

Step 1: Take given hexadecimal number

Step 2: Find the number of digits in the decimal

Step 3: If it has n digits, multiply each digit with 16n-1 where the digit is in the nth position

Step 4: Add the terms after multiplication

Step 5: The result is the decimal number equivalent to the given hexadecimal number. Now we have to convert this decimal to binary number.

Step 6: Divide the decimal number with 2

Step 7: Note the remainder

Step 8: Do the above 2 steps for the quotient till the quotient is zero

Step 9: Write the remainders in the reverse order.

Step 10: The result is the required binary number.

Hexa To Binary Examples

Question 1: Convert A2B16 to an equivalent binary number.

Solution: Given hexadecimal number = A2B16

First, convert the given hexadecimal to the equivalent decimal number.

A2B16 = (A × 162) + (2 × 161) + (B × 160)

= (A × 256) + (2 × 16) + (B × 1)

= (10 ×256) + 32 + 11

= 2560 + 43

= 2603(Decimal number)

Now we have to convert 260310 to binary

2 | 2603
2 |1301 -- 1
2 | 650 -- 1
2 | 325 -- 0
2 | 162 -- 1
2 | 81 -- 0
2 | 40 -- 1
2 | 20 -- 0
2 | 10 -- 0
2 | 5 -- 0
2 | 2 -- 1
2 | 1 -- 0
2 | 0 -- 1

Enter Caption

The binary number obtained is 1010001010112

Hence, A2B16 = 1010001010112

Question 2: Convert E16 to an equivalent binary number.

Solution: Given, a hexadecimal number is E.

First, convert the given hexadecimal to the equivalent decimal number.

E16 = E × 160

= E × 1

= E

=14 (Decimal number)

Now we have to convert 1410 to binary number.

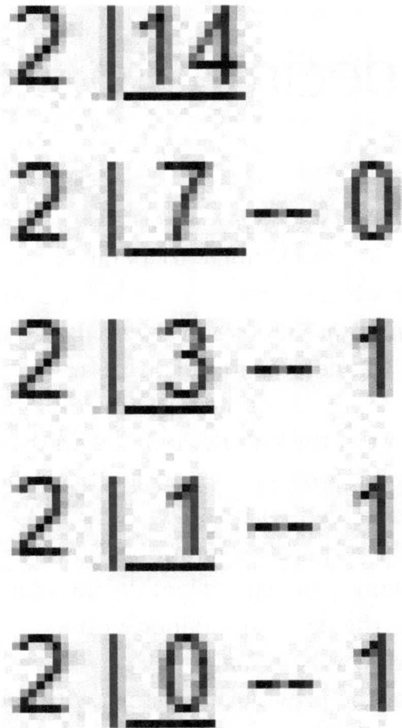

Enter Caption

The binary number obtained is 11102
Hence, E16 = 11102

CHAPTER EIGHTEEN

Hexadecimal to Octal

Hexadecimal to Octal Conversion

Conversion of hexadecimal to octal cannot be done directly. Firstly we need to convert hexadecimal into its equivalent decimal number then decimal to octal. Follow the steps below to understand the process.

step 1:Consider the given hexadecimal number

step2 :First count the number of digits in the number

step3 :If n is the position of the digit from the right end then multiply each digit with 16n-1

step4 :Add the terms after multiplication

step5: Resultant is the equivalent decimal form

step6: Divide the decimal number with 8

step7 :Note down the remainder

step8: Repeat the previous two steps with the quotient, until the quotient is zero

step9: Write the remainders in reverse order

step10:The obtained number is the required result

Example:

Convert 1BC16 into an octal number.

Solution: Given, 1BC16 is a hexadecimal number.

1 → 0001, B → 1011, C →1100

Now group them from right to left, each having 3 digits.

000, 110, 111, 100

000→0, 110 →6, 111→7, 100→4

Hence, 1BC16 = 6748

Hexadecimal	Octal	Equivalent Decimal	Equivalent Binary
0	0	0	0
1	1	1	1
2	2	2	10
3	3	3	11
4	4	4	100
5	5	5	101
6	6	6	110
7	7	7	111
8	10	8	1000
9	11	9	1001
A	12	10	1010
B	13	11	1011
C	14	12	1100
D	15	13	1101
E	16	14	1110

Hexadecimal to Octal Questions

Q.1: Find the equivalent octal form of C116.

Solution: Given, a hexadecimal number is C1

C116 = (C × 161) + (1 × 160)

= C × 16 + 1 × 1

=12 × 16 + 1

= 192 + 1

C116 =193 (Decimal form)

```
8 | 193
8 | 24  -- 1
8 | 3   -- 0
8 | 0   --3
```

The octal number is 3018
Hence, C116 = 3018.

CHAPTER NINETEEN

Hexadecimal to Decimal

The conversion of hexadecimal to decimal is done by using the base number 16. The hexadecimal digit is expanded to multiply each digit with the power of 16. The power starts at 0 from the right moving forward towards the right with the increase in power. For the conversion to complete, the multiplied numbers are added.

How to convert from hex to decimal

A regular decimal number is the sum of the digits multiplied with power of 10.

137 in base 10 is equal to each digit multiplied with its corresponding power of 10:

$13710 = 1\times102+3\times101+7\times100 = 100+30+7$

Hex numbers are read the same way, but each digit counts power of 16 instead of power of 10.

For hex number with n digits:

dn-1 ... d3 d2 d1 d0

Multiply each digit of the hex number with its corresponding power of 16 and sum:

decimal = dn-1×16n-1 + ... + d3×163 + d2×162 + d1×161+d0×160

Example #1

3B in base 16 is equal to each digit multiplied with its corresponding 16n:

3B16 = 3×161+11×160 = 48+11 = 5910

Example #2

E7A9 in base 16 is equal to each digit multiplied with its corresponding 16n:

E7A916 = 14×163+7×162+10×161+9×160 = 57344+1792+160+9 = 5930510

Example #3

0.8 in base 16:

0.816 = 0×160+8×16-1 = 0+0.5 = 0.510

Decimal Number System

A number system that uses digits from 0 to 9 to represent a number with base 10 is called the decimal number system. The number is expressed in base-10, where each value is denoted by 0 or the first nine positive integers. Each value in this number system has the place value of power 10. It means the digit at the tens place is ten times greater than the digit at the unit place.

Conversion from Hex to Decimal

As we know, number systems can be converted from one base to another. Thus, we can convert hexadecimal numbers to decimal easily. This number system conversion can be done as explained in the example given below:

Example:

Convert 7CF (hex) to decimal.

Solution:

Given hexadecimal number is 7CF.

In hexadecimal system,

7 = 7

C = 12

F = 15

To convert this into a decimal number system, multiply each digit with the powers of 16 starting from units place of the number.

7CF = (7 × 162) + (12 × 161) + (15 × 160)

= (7 × 256) + (12 × 16) + (15 × 1)

= 1792 + 192 + 15

= 1999

From this, the rule can be defined for the conversion from hex numbers to decimal numbers.

Suppose below is the hex number with n digits:

dn-1 ... d3 d2 d1 d0

Multiply each digit of the hex number with its corresponding powers of 16 and add them such as:

dn-1 × 16n-1 + ... + d3 × 163 + d2 × 162 + d1 × 161 + d0 × 160

Thus, the resultant number will be taken as base 10 or decimal number system.

dn-1 ... d3 d2 d1 d0 (hex) = dn-1 × 16n-1 + ... + d3 × 163 + d2 × 162 + d1 × 161 + d0 × 160 (decimal)

How to convert the hexadecimal number system to the decimal number system?

To convert the hexadecimal number system to the decimal number system, follow the below steps:

Step 1: Multiply each digit with the powers of 16 starting from the units place of the number.

Step 2: Simplify each of the products and add them.

Convert 7CA (hex) to decimal.

We know that 7 = 7, C = 12 and A = 10.

Therefore (7CA)16 = (7 × 162) + (12 × 161) + (10 × 160)

(7CA)16 = (7 × 256) + (12 × 16) + (10 × 1)

(7CA)16 = 1792+192+10

(7CA)16 = (1994)10

Hence, 7CA (hex) to decimal is 1994.

Convert 5BC (hex) to decimal.

We know that 5 = 5, B = 11 and C = 12.

Therefore (5BC)16 = (5 × 162) + (11 × 161) + (12 × 160)

(5BC)16 = (5 × 256) + (11 × 16) + (12 × 1)

(5BC)16 = 1280+176+12

(5BC)16 = (1468)10

Hence, 5BC (hex) to decimal is 1468.

9 798887 830490

Printed by Libri Plureos GmbH in Hamburg,
Germany